INTERNET

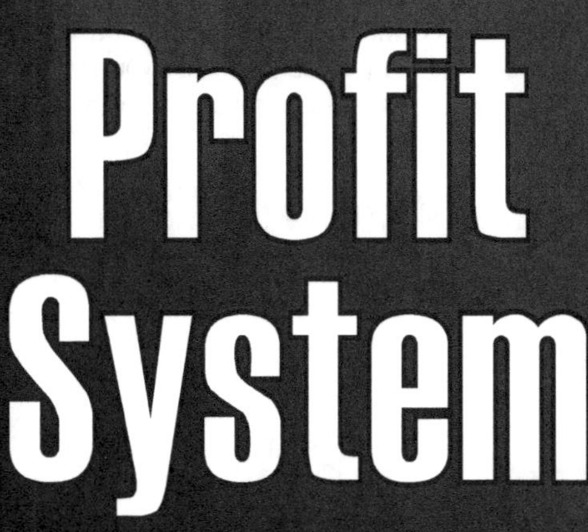

Profit
System

Introduction

Every entrepreneur has the power to make an absolute killing on the Internet.

Yes, this includes you.

Whether you're an existing marketer in search of serious passive income, a part-time dabbler who just can't get consistent sales with your existing funnel or maybe a newbie with no experience and a lot of desire, you have the power to pull six-figure profit off the Internet as consistent and routine as clockwork.

In fact, there is only one thing that separates the wannabes from the wealthy, the tinkerers from the Trumps: successful Internet marketers have learned how to effectively and consistently **DRIVE TRAFFIC** in an ever-changing Internet world.

It sounds simple, right? Well, it is. It's just not easy. It will require a journey toward personal and professional development to which you must totally commit. But why should you believe me? What's makes me such an expert on the subject?

I've spent twenty years building Internet businesses and creating software solutions that get results. My first Internet business began in 1997. In 2003 I launched a software company that generated profits in excess of $15,000 within 30 days and over six figures my first year.

I have developed innovative marketing tools, custom software solutions that drive tons of traffic. Internet marketing gurus swear by my software solutions and their effectiveness. I can tell you that everything you're about to read in this e-book *WORKS*. This is one of the most important skill sets you will ever learn.

This information will radically change your financial life and indirectly your entire life, given the correlation between financial success and personal freedom. It will give you control, once and for all, over how to achieve your short and long term goals. As a tool for financial independence it will ultimately impact every area of your life. Your confidence will soar.

As someone interested in Internet profits, you might very well have a goal in mind or some idea about what you want to do with this new-found knowledge. Perhaps you just want extra cash. Maybe you want to create wealth. Maybe you want to make enough profit to quit your current job and retire early. Maybe you just want to improve your marketing funnel.

Regardless of your intentions at this moment, I can tell you that as soon as you learn the skills I'm going to teach you, you are going to see immediate improvements in every area of your Internet marketing business.

Take a moment to consider why you do the things you do. What is the motivation that drives your actions? Why do you want to master Internet marketing?

Nine times out of ten the answer to that question will be: "If I can sell products on the Internet, I can make a lot of money." But can't you make a lot of money in a professional career? Think about it. A career as a nurse anesthetist requires about 6 years of education and offers a mean salary of about 140K on average throughout the United States. What about salesmen? There are door-to-door vacuum cleaner salesmen who make 100K per year.

Why isn't everyone knocking on doors and making a killing? Because not only is it difficult, there is no freedom in it. And worse, it is *IMPOSSIBLE TO LEVERAGE YOUR TIME AND EFFORT*. Careers which are the result of education and certification frequently result in some manner of 'glass ceiling' where future increased salaries (profit) isn't possible. On top of that you're tied into a burdensome weekly schedule.

The whole point of making money is freedom. Freedom to do what you want on your own time; freedom to live and work wherever you want, for as much or as little as you want.

That's it. That is the point. Don't get confused about why you are in college, or why you went to college or why you are working a career or just have a job. Everything you do, consciously or unconsciously, is to achieve the goal of quitting work for good and having enough money...to **DO WHAT YOU WANT**. And if you don't know the skills I'm about to teach you, then it doesn't matter how much you study or what you do. Nor does it matter how much money you make.

Not having the skills you are about to learn – how to properly and effectively create lasting value and drive traffic – means you won't have the confidence of knowing that you're heading in the proper direction; knowing that you'll be able to get what you want: financial independence.

There are lots of people out there who just get "lucky", but we are not interested in that. Why would you want to be one of the lucky ones? Why would you want to be the person who just so happened to be in the right place at the right time in order for something good to happen to you? I'm not going to teach you how to put yourself into routine strategies and systems which simply allow whatever happens to happen.

I'm going to teach you how to **CREATE** the most profitable and effective marketing systems, which will allow you to rapidly grow and scale your Internet business.

Everyone knows that "knowledge is power". I'm certain you've heard this phrase over and over throughout your life. It sounds good – but it is completely meaningless. Knowledge isn't power...

Application is power.

You can know anything and everything, but if you don't apply the concepts, you will not be any more powerful.

Let's say when you finish this e-book that I give you a system, which, if you use properly to plan and build a rock-solid Internet business, would generate a million dollars. All you have to do is follow the rules and it will only be a matter of time before you have a million dollars in profit.

When you get the system are you rich? Of course not. Do you have a million dollars? No, you don't! All you have is the knowledge about **HOW** to get the million dollars. You have to stand up and motivate yourself to follow the plan and get the money.

Therein lies the key to mastering this material. Knowledge is nothing more than a means to application - something that enables it. You are learning this material so it can be applied. If you don't use the knowledge you've gained, you're just taking up valuable space in your brain. You would be far better off just forgetting it altogether.

Are you still with me? Good. I want to mention a few more things about goals.

The human brain is an intention-fulfilling mechanism. We have the innate ability to create an idea about something we want and then work toward achieving it. Regardless of anything else, any external event, good or bad, we are always working toward the goals that we have created for ourselves.

As a result of this truth, it is extremely important to be aware of what your goals actually are. Your brain does not discern between what you might consider to be 'good' or 'bad' for you. If you imagine something, it takes that as a command to somehow get that specific thing.

This aspect of the human psyche is hard-wired into our most basic, innate cognitive processes. Think about your goals as an Internet marketer right now. Take some time to figure out exactly what you want to gain by learning this material.

Got it? I hope so. Be certain that it is something very specific. What you want is not as important as **WHY** you want it. Why do you want to learn how to effectively market products and services on the Internet? Why are you reading this e-book? You are much more likely to attain your goals if you can explain – with clarity – to yourself **WHY** you want them, not just what they happen to be.

Consider this very carefully. Tell me why you are learning this material or why you wish to learn it. Let me be clear. Whatever you wish to gain from this, you **WILL** gain in some manner at some point. If you do not uncover your true intentions and set proper goals accordingly, you will probably not be happy with what you attain. Remember, the human brain is a coping mechanism that does not discern, but merely attempts to fulfill intentions.

When I was learning the business, I thought I was very clear about what I wanted to get out of it. I wanted to be successful. The last thing I wanted was to be one of the seemingly massive statistics of people who fail at this business. But what I found out was that for me, just wanting success was not enough of a reason why – and a rather poor excuse for a goal.

Therefore, I was not ready for some of the early financial success that I achieved. Financial success has a way of creating its own issues resulting in circumstances we least expect.

So it goes with aspiring marketers more often than not. I've worked with many students who were not clear about their intentions from the beginning. They studied and applied knowledge and eventually found themselves at a point where they thought they wanted to be, only to realize that they weren't truly satisfied. They had nothing else to say other than they wanted to make money.

If that is your intention, if all you want to do is make money, it will happen. But the problem is that the moment you achieve that goal, you don't have anywhere else to go, nothing else to strive for. It can be generic and hollow. Your success will stall out and you will hit a ceiling.

There are lots of "experts" in this field – authors, consultants, marketers turned instructors, those who attempt to turn modest success into coaching businesses - who are not as successful at Internet marketing as they'd like you to think. They set out with the typical simple intention most marketers have: "I want to make some money". Now they have that ability but nothing else.

Or worse, they hop from one trend to the next, never understanding how to create **AUTHORITY**, **VALUE**, and **PASSIVE INCOME**.

They can make a living but have no idea how to transform the knowledge of Internet marketing into a larger business or wealth requisite to having true financial independence. Remember that you will pay tax on your profit, and if you're a full-time Internet marketer, you will have living expense. Some marketers who quit their careers for Internet 'fortune' do nothing more than trade one job for another.

Perhaps that doesn't sound like a bad idea – sitting around your house or condo near the beach pulling a living off the Internet. Hey, if that does it for you, then great! I'm not judging it. But you must be certain of your true intentions because what they may be, I can guarantee that you are going to fulfill them.

I know this from experience. I was one of those guys who just wanted to make money. Personally, when I hit that target, it was pretty hollow. I figured I needed to do more. More systems, more software, more everything. I thought I needed to spend even more *TIME* and *MONEY* to increase my bottom line. Had I realized that my true intentions were much larger – about the overall picture of personal freedom and financial independence, I could have saved a lot of time and avoided a lot of frustration.

I've worked with enough different types of personalities and preferences to begin to see patterns in behavior as well as business-specific patterns. These core tenets and strategies transcend time and 'change'. These are the concepts that I'm going to be teaching you.

The reality is that **90% of Internet startups FAIL in 120 days**. It gets worse. Statistical probabilities do not favor success for most because the entrepreneur is part of the PROBLEM.

Wildly successful entrepreneurs all exhibit the same characteristic: they are masters of time and resource management. I will show you how to do this. You will not achieve that end just by reading this e-book, however. You will need to combine the knowledge herein with sufficient personal growth and experience.

This e-book is a primer for identifying a simple formula for generating six-figure income. Keep it handy so you can refer to it as necessary.

Maybe you're still not convinced. Are you still making the excuse that because you were not born with inherent talent or a ton of business acumen you won't ever be good at it?

The thing about successful entrepreneurs is that they are seldom born and almost always made. You see it everywhere. People who enjoyed success in other areas of life are often brought to their knees in business. Easy access to the Internet lowers the barrier to entry. This is both positive and negative. It is phenomenal that average people can make above average incomes, but only if they understand key business structures and processes that consistently produce success.

What I'm saying is that great marketers are not born with the ability to master the necessary skills – they're learned. The skill set has to be acquired. It may not be learned by reading an e-book or studying a course, but that doesn't mean the learning process didn't happen.

Many 'natural' entrepreneurs acquire invaluable information by mimicking successful marketers. This is only thing that separates you from the naturals. Just remember that these naturals don't know why they're doing something. They work on a subconscious level. If you don't know why something works, it's because you are not aware of it. Therefore, it seems to be natural.

In terms of evolution, being a natural is not an adaptive trait. It will not help them survive in the long run. High-flying Internet marketers fly and crash all the time. I once lost $100,000 on a deal gone bad. Outcomes can be random. But long term success is grounded in the ability to create value and drive traffic consistently throughout your enterprise.

This is exactly how I have generated seven-figure money in my career. And now you are going to learn how to have the same level of success by acting on a totally conscious level. You will be able to control your actions when it comes to the process or learning and implementation. You will therefore be able to control subsequent outcomes. That's exciting!

The concept of learning in this manner is so much more powerful than having a traditional 'natural' ability or learning 'naturally'. So when things occasionally don't go as planned or you hit a bump, you'll know how to fix it. Naturals in this case would be forced to give up and move on. There are lots of entrepreneurs and Internet marketers from the tech-boom in the early 2000s who are teaching elementary school in the Midwest.

Me? I know I have the skills to adapt to ever-changing conditions.

Here is an example: most people drive a car without ever understanding how the car actually works. Only mechanics and engineers truly understand how a car functions. So, when your car breaks down, if you're not a mechanic, you must call someone who is one so they can fix it. But if you are a mechanic, you can simply assess the damage and make the repair.

Entrepreneurialism is a lot different than automobile mechanics, but learning how to effectively market is quite similar. If you understand the core Internet marketing 'mechanics', you will be able to make "repairs" and build businesses more successfully than your competitors.

Use the concepts in this e-book to structure your business properly. Test out the systems on your own. I've tested these strategies hundreds of times over the years. Other entrepreneurs have learned these strategies and continue to test them. Up to this point I have worked out every possible kink that I could find. Over the years I've built dozens of business strategies based on the very principles you'll find here.

The best benefit this information can offer you is the ability to really make these strategies your 'own'. Once you own them and discover the limitations and unlimited possibility therein (as well as your own potential), you become conscious of what is going on in your business and in your head. And that is a great place to be. Plain and simple, this stuff works.

While you read on, keep an open mind. The process and everything you are about to learn is going to change your life in ways you haven't even imagined yet. Herein you will find important tools for how to make a killing off the Internet.

The World Has Changed

And it will never be the same. Ever.

Following World War II, Americans were flush with cash from the post-war boom. The American 'Dream' was born; derived from a Fannie Mae government marketing campaign aimed at the well-employed middle class. It spawned the mortgage industry. Why live within your means when you could borrow for the dream house in the suburbs?

And then it happened. A concept that built the great American nation, 'work to save', turned into 'borrow to spend'. Eventually the 15 trillion-dollar mortgage banking industry stream rolled the entire nation, promising a quick and easy solution to 'keeping up with the Joneses'.

This evolution was accompanied by the largest systematic banking intervention in history through the Federal Reserve. The longer it lasted, the more pronounced the boom-and-bust cycles became. Cheap money flooded the housing and financial markets.

A rising tide lifts all the boats, so consumer spending increased commensurately thanks again to the banking industry, now flush with mortgage interest profits. Credit card debt went parabolic, ballooning from a mere $700 billion in 2005 to $2.5 trillion by 2007.

It was a house of cards…

That came tumbling down in 2008 with an unprecedented financial crisis that rocked the world. The most interesting component about this latest bust was that in every similar historical debacle the middle class was able to absorb the shock. Why? It collectively carried the largest tax burden and so was the largest source of income. It also spends the most.

But this time the credit cards were maxed out. The kicker was that in succeeding years the job and housing markets remained flat. Uh-oh.

So what was left?

Increasing national debt.

The government-sponsored bail out of the banks whereby newly printed cash was used to pay interest on bank assets, keeping the entire industry afloat. Trillions of dollars were added to the national debt. The result?

The recession never ended for most Americans. Let's take a look at the numbers:

- 25% of American households say they are 'just getting by' financially
- 13% are 'finding it difficult' to get by
- 34% feel worse off than they did five (5) years ago
- Only 30% report they are better off financially than five (5) years ago

And even a closer look...

The cost of higher education is making many Americans reconsider the traditional 4-year education. Soaring tuition is out-pacing inflation yearly.

The American obsession with automobiles has raced to record levels. In the last year, the average length of an auto loan is now 66 months, the highest level ever. More disconcerting is that 25% of all new vehicle loans originated now extend 73 months to (I hope you're sitting down) 84 months. Seven years! The price of an average auto sale is now $27,612 with a record high payment of $474.

The borrowing continues on unprecedented scales. But meanwhile...

Home ownership rates are dropping, to 64.7%, the lowest level in nineteen (19) years. Go figure rents are on the rise, increasing 6.1% on a year-over-year basis as of this writing. Can we count on rising home values to bail out the debt? Maybe not this time.

The savings picture adds clarity. 26% of Americans do not have a single cent set aside for emergency expenses. 67% have less than six (6) months of expenses saved. Curiously, high wage-earning households with incomes in excess of 75K per year are no better off. Fewer than half (46%) have a six (6) month savings cushion.

It gets worse. 36% of Americans have nothing saved for retirement. That same 36% have less than $1,000 in savings and investments in the checking account. Why? The cost of living of course. Government intervention favors inflation over it's much less desirable counterpart, deflation.

The bottom line is that the nation's wealth has been decimated thanks to a combination of falling stock markets and housing prices over the last decade. The recent median net worth totaled just $56,335 down 36% from $87,992 in 2003.

And the big shocker: the only demographic which reported an increase in wealth during the same period was the 90th percentile (the richest top 10% of Americans).

People are broke.

Rising income and wealth inequality has been on the increase for the past several decades; the trend is unlikely to reverse anytime soon.

The most likely scenario: the slow recovery from the 2008 Great Recession will continue to create inequality in the coming years as assets are drawn down to cover increased consumption costs.

And so you might be asking: "Is there a silver-lining *ANYWHERE,* Jeff?

Yes. There is. Right here: despite all the statistics about what is happening to the masses, contradictions to the trend are *EVERYWHERE!* **More people than ever have discovered personal freedom as well as financial success** while *real* unemployment (or underemployment) probably exceeds 20% or more.

People just like me. A surfer turned DJ turned eight-figure Internet marketer. I am one of the 10% who experience increased wealth since 2003. My business expanded twenty fold.

Contrary to what you might think, none of what you just read about the changing world is bad news. It's simply the new reality. It's time to carve your **OWN** path. It's time to build a rock-solid business that will generate passive income *AND* furnish personal freedom.

And your best bet for accomplishing this goal is to join a team with a proven track record of success. More on this in just a minute.

But first... you are going to have to make a choice.

Why You Must Choose <u>YOU</u>

The choice you must first make is YOU.

James Altucher said it best:

"Human beings are born pioneers. The rise of corporatism (as opposed to capitalism) forced people into cubicles instead of out into the world, exploring and inventing and manifesting. The ethic of the Choose Yourself era is to not depend on those stifling trends that are defeating you. Instead, **build your own platform**, have faith and confidence in yourself instead of a jury-rigged system, and **define success on your own terms**."

Defining success on your own terms. Think about it.

Not societal norms, conventional wisdom or whatever popular culture dictates.

Since the dawn of man's time on earth, the basic human drive has been to seek out frontiers. Consider the great migrations, manifest destiny, crossing the Bering Strait, early European exploration, colonization, refugeeism, breaking the sound barrier, one-hundred story buildings, a walk on the moon, the Wright brothers and aviation, nanotechnology, splitting the atom, finite mathematics, the artificial heart. I could go on. It's everywhere in history. It's everywhere right now, right in front of us.

Even the Pilgrims did it. They chose themselves. The hallmark of the human evolutionary spirit has been to carve out our own path, our own method – our own truth.

The Burger King Restaurant chain built an international brand around "**have it your way**".

It's time to return to that way of thinking.

Choosing yourself will give you the skill set required to go out into the world and dictate your place in it.

It isn't just about starting an Internet business because you want to make money. The 'choose yourself' mindset must first be in place because it furnishes the self-mastery required to put yourself out there and build the rock-solid business of your dreams.

Without a conscious decision to choose yourself, setbacks may seem insurmountable, or you will ultimately succumb to the eroding middle class and ever-shrinking median incomes.

Choosing yourself isn't a selfish thing. It's not self-centeredness. What you learn is that grounding yourself first, deciding what you want and following your destiny derives from relative self-mastery. It's a foundation for attacking your goals and following your dreams from the perspective of a healthy, sane, complete sense of self.

This basis allows you to act in harmony with your environment and those most important in your life. You won't 'burn out'. You'll seldom be bored. Life won't get stale. In this respect choosing you is the best possible precursor to not only creating a meaningful life, but also taking the best care of your family and your circle of influence.

It's the ultimate value creator. And value is the supreme metric. People will be drawn to you and what you offer. And they will gladly exchange money for it, enriching you *AND* them.

The divorce courts are full of people who thought they were choosing themselves. They thought they were following their own path and walking their truth. But they weren't. All they did was buy into some canned conventional 'dream' without ever knowing who they are. These are the people who wake up one day, look at the husband or the wife, the kids, the house, the pressure, relentless financial obligations, college tuition, debt, the $800 Lexus payment and think, "I'm *DONE*."

If you develop the mindset that you and you alone are responsible for carving out your place in the world, you can then focus on the idea that creating sincere value will open up all the doors you need.

And that's when the money starts rolling in. Trust me, it will.

At every turn in my career and business evolution, I chose myself. I wasn't even aware of it at the beginning. The reality is that the choices I made for myself were ultimately choices made for my family, my future, my way of life. The foundation of my entire empire rests on that very first choice: Me. I can tell you first hand, it *WORKS*. One of its greatest benefits has been the ability to guide other entrepreneurs in the proper direction.

Think you are ready to choose? Let's get down to business.

Introducing The 3-Step Plan

Let's simplify the process by beginning with the bottom line.

If you want to make six figures annually on the Internet, you are only going to require two things:

(1) An offer... and...
(2) Someone to buy it.

It really is that simple. It's just not easy. But most people make the process much more difficult than it has to be.

If all you do is focus on this simple structure of offer + buyer everything else will fall in line.

Remember that the only difference between Internet millionaires and those who never make a dime is that the millionaire was able to get lots of people to purchase a product or service.

Let's look at how we are going to work with this structure using a 3-step plan:

1. **Building An Audience.** All successful businesses are built on the foundation of establishing, engaging and expanding a community with similar interests. Think of this audience as your 'tribe'.

2. **Building A Relationship...** with that audience. People will know, like and trust you enough to do business with you. This is the foundation for creating AUTHORITY. The result is social proof.

3. **Creating A Sales Machine...** to offer high-quality, valuable products and services to your audience.

Now let's examine each step of this process in more detail...

Step 1: Building An Audience

Always remember this fundament truth:

Here are five (5) ways to effectively build your audience:

(1) **LIST.** This is an email database of subscribers who 'opt-in' to receive communication from you on a regular basis. Typically, you will create a free offer to entice people to join your list. You will have to provide sufficient value in order to do this. Then you can begin to send follow-up emails to your subscriber base. More on this in just a minute.

(2) **BLOG.** This is a time-based website which posts content on a continuous basis. A blog is superior to a generic (static) website because frequent updating and 'backlinks' facilitate improved rankings in search engines. Don't worry if you are not familiar with these terms. You will be soon. A blog is an excellent portal for establishing VALUE and AUTHORITY.

(3) **VIDEO.** Using popular sites such as Youtube, you create and post videos on a 'channel' where people can subscribe to receive notification of your updates and new posts.

(4) **PODCASTS.** This technique involves offering downloadable audio series. Generally, podcasts are schedule weekly (or twice a week), and cover topics of interest to your audience.

(5) **SOCIAL MEDIA.** Here you create a digital 'following' on platforms such as Facebook, Twitter or Instagram. Also included are Facebook 'fan' pages which focus on specific topics and provide value via frequent posting and interaction with your tribe.

You do not have to use all five of these strategies, but ultimately you can if your business and interests deem it necessary.

For the purposes of this blueprint, I'm going to focus on the **LIST** and **BLOG** as the cornerstone of your strategy.

List building will be your primary objective at the beginning. Using the tools I'm about to provide, you can be up and running – collecting emails address today!

List Building

The cornerstone of effective Internet marketing is the development of the email list. This is how you will be able to achieve high customer retention and high lifetime value.

What most marketers overlook is timing. Email address acquisition *AFTER* the sale is too late, because it requires the customer to pass through the pay wall and current sales funnel. Therefore, your list will only be comprised of paying customers.

But what about the 'tire-kickers'? And those potential customers who are either curious or simply shopping?

You don't to miss out on *ANYONE* who expresses an interest in your niche. Think of it as an opportunity to introduce yourself, provide **VALUE** and demonstrate your **AUTHORITY**.

From this perspective, you must always list-build first. If you learn one thing from this entire blueprint, it should be this. As you will see, your list is your business. Outside the world of Internet marketing, this same phenomenon can be seen in commercial sales and marketing.

Have you ever seen the same people, perhaps you are included in this group, at your local Starbucks? You know, the same ones who make it a daily habit to stop for their favorite drink? This group is part of the millions of people on the Starbucks 'list'. It's that sector of current and potential customers that are *most likely* to purchase from Starbucks in the very near future.

The technical term for this concept is called **MARKET REACH**. I teach Internet marketing students how to best employ this tool. On the Internet, where you don't have a physical store, your email list is basically the same thing as that group of Starbucks enthusiasts.

With this in mind, let's examine my primary list building strategy:

- Build email list PRIOR to sending traffic to the sales page.
- Provide **VALUE** in exchange for the email address (this is generally an information product such as an e-E-book or video course). We will discuss this 'freebie' next.
- Create a free **SQUEEZE PAGE** to give away the product and capture emails (You may also use an Opt-In box on a website or a **BLOG)**.
- Run traffic to the squeeze page or blog.
- Locate affiliate products to promote according to your pre-determined **FUNNEL.**

I will be discussing the funnel later in this blueprint. But first, we need to cover sequences and an overview of the tools just mentioned so you know exactly what to do.

The Follow-up Sequence

Sequences are the series of emails with which you will correspond with your new potential customer via email once they have joined your list. This sounds complicated but it's not. There are software tools that can help you automate the process.

Keep in mind, that from the very beginning, you want to provide VALUE and demonstrate AUTHORITY. There are two areas of focus:

- **Content**
- **Frequency**

Content is just that – exactly what you are trying to introduce or discuss. Frequency is all about how often you email list members.

The best strategy is to systematically bundle free value and promotions for either your affiliate links or your own products. I will demonstrate how to do this shortly. For now, just consider the importance of list building and the follow-up sequence as your primary focus.

Once you do this everything else falls in line. Let's look at the tools you'll require.

Tools

To facilitate your list building initiative you'll need an autoresponder service to first collect email addresses and then blast your follow-up sequences.

The ticket is that all of this is automation. Time-based email scheduling will enable you to engage each new list member with your follow-up sequence beginning on the very first day they join the list.

This is incredibly powerful as you can imagine. My favorite autoresponder service is Aweber.

Once your email autoresponder is in place, you'll require either squeeze pages or an opt-in box to collect the email addresses.

Here's an example of a basic squeeze page...

You'll also want to consider employing an opt-in box on a website or blog. Most autoresponder services have tools for building and customizing squeeze pages and opt-in boxes. This further simplifies the process.

I'll cover some more detail about list building when I discuss blogging later in the e-book. This has been a good introduction to the concepts of list building and follow-up sequences as well as the tools required to facilitate these strategies.

Let's review the benefits of this strategy:

- You build strong **LIFETIME VALUE** across your enterprise. This is the possibility of repeat customers because you have earned their trust.
- You create exceptional **VALUE.** Delivering timely, pertinent information to your Audience (filling a need) is something your list subscribers will not be able to find elsewhere.
- You achieve solid **CUSTOMER RETENTION** rates.
- You build a rock-solid long term business…by first building the **LIST**

I've made as much as $75,000 in just a few days with targeted email marketing. The secret is found in the promotion of higher priced products further down the sales funnel. You'll be learning the best way accomplish this objective later in this blueprint.

Why You Need A BLOG

In this chapter, I'll discuss one of the most important tools available to successfully create the powerful long-term Internet business you've been learning about in this blueprint.

That tool is the Blog.

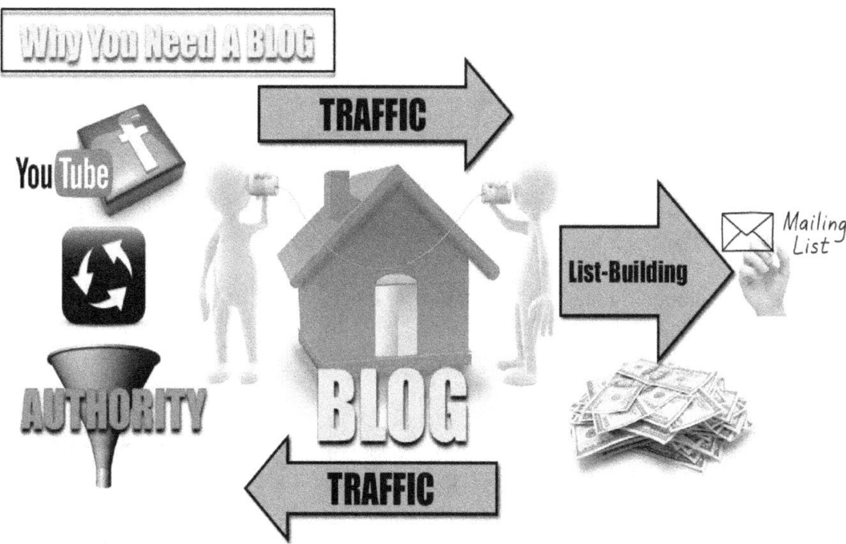

Think of a blog as your home-base on the Internet. It is a powerful communication portal connecting you to the world. It is a place where you can connect with customers, potential customers and students. It is a destination that allows you to introduce your business and establish authority.

The blog enables you integrate social networking, traffic generating tools, and most importantly, it allows you to build your list.

It's always employing the proper mix of content, marketing and monetization to create authority. When you build an authority blog and combine this with a large email list, you have a viable business entity that can be further monetized and sold.

What most marketers don't understand is that a blog must have a specific layout and theme that makes it a viable commercial entity. Therefore, how the blog is initially setup and structured is very important to your success.

As if there aren't enough pitfalls for most aspiring Internet marketers, the learning curve for successful blogging is sufficiently steep that many newbies and professionals alike are deterred from blogging and miss out on a huge opportunity to create a high-traffic business.

An authority-style blog layout will enable you to effectively build a list with an 'opt-in' box to collect email address and further introduce customers and potential customers (leads) to your business and top portion of your sales funnel.

A properly-established blog requires the following:

- **Web hosting**
- **Domain name**

For hosting, I recommend Bluehost because it is one of the most affordable and reliable services available. They also give you a free domain name when you sign up. Bluehost also includes a 1-Click WordPress install, so you can easily install your blogging platform in only a few minutes.

Here's a great video on how to start a profitable blog:

https://www.youtube.com/watch?v=5ZrLIhP2zy0

I suggest watching the entire video and completing each step on your own blog as you follow along in the video. That way you can have your blog set up correctly within a few hours, so you can start posting content and getting free traffic.

Now that you are familiar with the tools of list building and the blog, let's examine how you can effectively build a rock-solid relationship with the new members recently acquired on your list.

Step 2: Building A Relationship

Let's take a look at another fundamental business truth:

Higher conversion rates on offers to your existing audience (list) are proven. Conversion rates through advertisements to 'cold' prospects will always underperform in comparison.

This is why it is imperative that you establish a quality relationship with your audience.

The easiest solution is to provide a high-demand freebie first as a lead magnet to attract new prospects to your list. Once there, you will continue to offer freebies – inter-mixed with offers and promotions as a way to create value and build the relationship.

A freebie will enable you to:

(1) Introduce your expertise to your audience.
(2) Promote offers to your audience.

A great tactic for number 2 above is to use a 'blending' technique which positions promotional offers inside free value-driven content. You will be able to engage your audience with ways to address their pain-points while offering solutions with products and services that make you money.

Following are examples of freebies that I have used over the years with solid success:

Articles or blog posts. Articles can include just about any style or concept such as 'how-to', overviews, tips, tactics, strategies or anything else of interest to your audience. This is why it is important to know your audience, especially their pain-points. Articles are a great way to engage your audience and deliver honest value.

Reports. Reports are similar to articles but offer more structure and are greater in length. Focus on one specific problem or issue with each report. Prospects who absorb this content and find it use are very likely to become customers. For example, you might write a nutrition report that tells dieters exactly what to eat to slim down and start feeling better.

Toolkits. This freebie makes it easy for your prospects to take action on the information they've been learning about. For example, a business start-up toolkit might include template for fliers or mailings, sales forms or invoices.

Webinars. Your audience will place a high value on live events. This makes webinars an attractive freebie. The added benefit is that webinar recordings can be used as marketing tools. If you cannot manage a webinar on your own or lack sufficient content, you may explore partnering with an affiliate. More on this later.

Case studies. This tactic provides information or details a plan about how to achieve a specific result. Because of the added benefit of social proof and inspiration, case studies are a proven tool to help promote a specific offer. For example, you can provide a case study showing how a marketer increased traffic using one specific strategy.

Email courses. I know several marketers who specialize in autoresponder email courses. The benefits of multi-part training segments as a freebie is that you do not have to create all the content before you can deliver value to your audience. Furthermore, over time you will be training your list subscribers to anticipate your value. Try this example: a 10-part e-course called "The 10 Secrets for Quickly Tripling Your Internet Traffic", sent via autoresponder on a schedule of 1-2 segments per week.

Cheat sheets. I use cheat sheets all the time to condense a more complex task down to a manageable procedure. Usually just one page, cheat sheets are downloadable, printable PDFs that provide exceptional value. They are also evergreen and may be included with other offers or as additional content in your autoresponder.

Newsletters. Probably one of the best tactics for interacting with your audience, newsletters can be sent on a weekly basis. Content can vary from training segments to human interest to industry news and product reviews, or anything that allows you to connect with your tribe. Autoresponders such as Aweber enable you to create great looking html templates so your newsletter appears professional and hip.

Interviews. One of the best ways to build social proof and inspire your audience is the interview. Interview success stories are a phenomenal way to connect with people, build your brand, and encourage your audience to take action. Interviews combine social proof with value – a powerful 1-2 punch.

In order to make the most of the freebie, you will need to know a few things first before you decide which strategies to use and how to structure your campaigns.

8 Proven Steps to Maximizing Your Freebies

#1: High-Quality Content

Without a doubt your freebies must be high-quality. Try to focus on one specific issue or problem with a method, strategy or advice that gets results. Keep it short and to the point.

Some of the best content is that which is simple yet effective. Consider the "Try this one easy thing" approach.

#2: Make It Useful

Your freebie must be something that your audience is craving. This is why market research is paramount. You must know who you are dealing with so you can properly engage them and improve their circumstance.

The best way to do this is a combination of market research and surveys. We've discussed this before but autoresponders are a great way to include surveys which will you sniff our audience demand. Then you can create valuable content for both freebies and paid promotions.

Never forget the axiom about filling a need. If you can help something look better, feel better or make more money, you will be a friend for life. More on this later when we discuss the product funnel in detail.

#3: Make It Personal

You will notice that most well-known industry experts or marketers put a face with the content. By this I mean that you allow your audience to get to know you – what you look like as well as personal details that allow them to connect with you on a more intimate level.

The importance of this bond cannot be overstated. Adding personal details such as tidbits about your everyday life, preferences and goals can go a long way to building the bond.

Putting a face on your brand is one of the best ways to build it. List subscribers will come to recognize you and look for your value-added content.

#4: Empathize

No one likes to be 'sold' anything. High pressure sales gimmicks and over-the-top offers will not build the bond you are seeking for long-term success. Your audience needs to know that you understand their pain points.

Let your audience know that you are aware of how they are feeling or where they are on a specific journey. Perhaps you have been there yourself. Empathy is the ultimate connector. When your list sees you as 'one of us', your honest credibility will skyrocket.

#5: Social Proof

Although these tips are not in any specific order, social proof is probably the most important tool in your arsenal. It also makes perfect use of the freebie.

Testimonials from your audience are one of the best ways to build your brand and expand your influence. The Internet is filled with bogus offers, extreme promotions and unbelievable stories. Honest review and testimonials will set you apart and give you much needed credibility.

Testimonials and reviews should be specific and include detail about how someone was able to benefit or achieve a certain goal.

#6: Case Studies

Use case studies to as a method for building credibility and maximizing social proof.

Recently, I conducted several case studies for traffic-generating software using a small group of clients who had recently purchased the product.

This focus group provided specific details about how their businesses improved during the 2-week testing phase after they implemented the software. These results were then published in a newsletter.

If you do not conduct your own case studies, you might try publishing existing case studies in your industry or niche. It is one of the best ways to maximize the freebie.

#7: Engagement

The importance of proper engagement with your audience is crucial to your success. You must always answer questions and respond to comments promptly.

Be certain to add value with invested answers and sincere empathy. This is a great opportunity to teach, direct and encourage your audience.

If one of your list members is the catalyst for an interview, training segment or newsletter topic, be certain to include their name in the process. This builds loyalty and makes you accessible.

I work with one marketer who uses this tactic all the time. He does a weekly Q&A (question and answer) segment in a newsletter where he personally responds to a subscriber's question. What a powerful tool! It builds credibility and social proof at the same time.

Be certain to factor engagement into your business. Allow for a certain amount of time each week to respond to questions and comments. Some of the most successful marketers and content providers I know have a policy that no question goes unanswered.

One of the most demoralizing things you can do to a member of your audience is ignore them. You would be surprised at how often this happens with Internet businesses.

Marketers are so busy marketing that they forget the most important thing of all – the needs of their audience.

#8: Maintain a 3:1 Ratio of Freebie to Promotion

It has been proven that high unsubscribe rates comes from two things: over-promotion and excessive email frequency.

You will have to balance the amount of your interaction as well as a ratio of free content to paid promotions.

If the only time your audience hears from you is when you have a new promotion or some other product for them to purchase, they will tire quickly and begin to suspect your business. This is not how you build trust.

Try this: for every 1 promotion that you send to your list, be sure to include 3 freebies. These should flow naturally from week to week and may include a survey, article, video or any of the other value-added content I mentioned.

Your autoresponder sequence should have a natural flow. People do not mind purchasing products and services that help them solve a problem or fill a need. This will occur naturally as you interweave free valuable content with offers.

Now that we have studied how to maximize the relationship with our list, let's move on the most exciting part: building a sales machine which benefits from all the work we have done to provide value.

Step 3: Creating A Sales Machine

Now we come to the part you have been anticipating: monetizing your business. We want to take the shortest path to turning the list and a good relationship with our audience into six-figure revenue.

The best way to do this is by creating your own products or partnering with content creators who fill a key, in-demand niche.

This way you control the quality of the information you produce in addition to controlling the list and how you engage with your audience.

What you will be doing is building a 'funnel' that includes are variety of products at various price points to engage your audience at wherever they are most likely to commit financially.

The process begins with the freebie and graduates successively through a series of higher and higher-priced products.

As your audience continues to get to know and trust you more, they will commit to purchasing these products.

At any one time, you will have a group of devoted followers who truly respond to your content. This group is worth gold. In a coming chapter I will show you exactly how this funnel works.

For now, check out five examples of how easy it can be to achieve your financial goal of 6-figure income:

> **Example 1:** Create a $27 a month membership site. You need 310 active members to earn $100,440 per year.
>
> **Example 2:** Sell a $77 video training info product. You need 4 sales per day to make $112,420 per year.
>
> **Example 3:** Provide a $197 "done for you" service. You need 10 sales per week to make $102,440 per year.
>
> **Example 4:** Create a $997 webinar. You need 17 sales per webinar (6 webinars a year) to make $101,694 per year.
>
> **Example 5:** Set up a $4,997 private 12-week coaching program. You need 21 sales to make $104,937 per year.

As you will see in the next chapter, the process can be simple. The best part is that you can start right now and very quickly build a successful Internet business.

I will show you exactly how to take consistent, month-by-month steps to improve conversions, get more and more traffic, and add products to your funnel.

Some of my students have used the exact same funnel you are about to learn to build million-dollar Internet businesses.

They didn't have any special skills or expertise. Neither did I when I got started. Literally anyone can do this... even YOU.

So, I hope you're excited and ready to take action!

Let's learn all everything we need to know about a funnel...

The Sales Funnel

Many new Internet marketers make the mistake of focusing on a specific product or promotion at the expense of the long term big picture. Even experienced entrepreneurs make a similar error.

You have to begin to think about your business as an enterprise. Depending on your niche, what are all the various types of products and services you can present to both your current and prospective customers. Think value.

Your subscriber has joined your list because they are looking to solve a problem or fill some need. Successful Internet marketers know how to effectively meet demand either by innovation or coupling the customer with an existing effective product or service via affiliate promotions.

I'm always reminded of a quote I heard from a seven-figure marketer early in my career:

> **"IF YOU CAN TEACH PEOPLE HOW TO FEEL BETTER, LOOK YOUNGER, BE THINNER OR _GET RICH_, THE WORLD WILL BEAT A PATH TO YOUR DOOR."**

Taking this concept one step further, let's consider a concept called **MARKET REACH**. Think of 'reach' as the universe of potential clients or customers for your particular niche, product or service.

You want to make the most of this demographic by delivering value across a broad spectrum of engagement depending on how great the problem or need is for the customer or potential customer. You achieve this goal through your enterprise funnel.

In this chapter we'll expand on the concept of the funnel I mentioned earlier in the e-book.

Examine the following image:

The sales funnel model works in any niche market. Notice how the funnel addresses the concerns of the market interested in a specific type of product with a wide variety of solutions (in terms or price and extent), depending on how great the demand for a solution may be for any given customer. This is KEY!

This funnel, the proper sequence of widget products and service, accomplishes several tasks:

- It introduces your concept or idea of the widget FREE of charge – this will enable you to build your **LIST**.
- Keeps start-up costs low – **you grow your funnel as your business grows.**
- Next, as customers and potential customers become more acquainted with your business and perceive its value, the funnel will help build your **BRAND**.
- Your business will benefit from 'Social Proof' generated not only by your customers who have experience value, but also from your own branded success.
- Next, as customers move through the funnel, benefiting from the more advanced widget solutions provide, the funnel builds high lifetime value.

The Hyper-Responsive List Group

As your business expands, whether you are promoting your own products or affiliate products and services, there will be a select group of customers who will become your raving fans and love what you have to offer.

This group will purchase virtually everything you promote because you have earned their trust by providing sincere value. This same group will make it ways through the funnel to either additional, higher-priced products or higher-priced widget products in the same niche.

This is called the 'Hyper-Responsive' List group. These customers create high lifetime value because they will purchase products and services at the bottom of the funnel.

This is where most marketers make the mistake of only promoting cheaper, niche-introductory products. Remember, credibility and a brand must be built. Trust must be earned.

USE THE FREE REPORT AND LESS EXPENSIVE PRODUCTS AT THE TOP OF THE FUNNEL TO INTRODUCE YOUR EXPERTISE, CREATE VALUE AND **BUILD YOUR LIST!**

This way, you don't have to work so hard to acquire new customers and increase your monthly sales totals. The flow will occur automatically.

Remember that the funnel is scalable to virtually any business model, whether you are creating your own information products or promoting affiliate products and services.

With this in mind, take a look at 3 proven ways to increase your business...

1. Get more customers. There are two ways to do this. The first way is to get more targeted traffic. The second way is to track and test all your campaigns and landing pages, so that you're converting more of your browsers to buyers.

2. Get more customers to spend more per sale. In other words, increase your profit per transaction. You can do this by offering upsells, cross-sells and one-time offers on your order form. This will also occur naturally as customers work their way through your expanding funnel.

3. Get more customers to spend more per sale more often. One of the keys to the big profits in your business is how often you can get your existing customers to buy from you repeatedly. That's why it's so important to keep adding products to your funnel, so you that you have larger products and services to offer your hyper-responsive list group.

Now let's condense everything into one easy, actionable plan you can start implementing TODAY!

Are You Willing To Choose YOU?

Believe it or not, you now possess everything you need to know to build a wildly successful Internet business. Perhaps some of the details are fuzzy, but that is OK. The point is that from the perspective of structure, you know exactly what to do:

> (1) Build an Audience...
> (2) Create a rock-solid relationship with that Audience...
> (3) Build and expand a round-the-clock sales machine with a sales funnel.

Take the process step by step, day after day, building your business like a brick layer builds a massive wall.

You can imagine your 6-figure business at its completion, but do not be overwhelmed by the process it will take to get there.

I am going to give you a specific starting point – right now. You can start today to build the business of your dreams.

Do this...

One list + one source of traffic + one freebie or targeted offer

Use the tools mentioned earlier in the e-book. If you take this first step you will have a list provider so you can begin to collect email addresses for your future funnel.

Each day, every month, take one step closer to completing your funnel. This could be a new product, finding a new source of traffic to add to your list, or even adding a new freebie to your autoresponder to create more value and build your relationship and brand.

The choice to begin TODAY is a choice for you. Will you do it? Or will you make an excuse to put off your Internet business for another time?

If you begin today you will be amazed at the progress you have made in three months, six months or even a year.

Your focus on list building will drive your business as you find out how to fill the needs of your audience. You will learn their pain points and what products and services will improve their lives, improve their health or help make them more money.

They will love you for it, and in return you will profit handsomely.

This is the sure way. This is the process of creating value.

It remains the most powerful strategy I have ever seen. I can tell you it works. I have done it. I'm doing it right now and I'm teaching others how to live their dreams.

If you apply everything you've learned in this e-book and use the tools I've provided, you will achieve great success on the Internet. You now have a proven **SYSTEM**.

There is no need to struggle any more with trial-and-error or hit-and-miss Internet marketing opportunities.

It is time to choose you for all the reasons I've suggested in this e-book. It's about defining success on your own terms, carving your own path and creating a lifestyle for you and those you care about just like I did.

To **YOUR** success!